Chickens For Kids: Pecking Through the Facts

Cluck Into The World of Chickens with Fun Facts, Amazing Photos, And Everything You Need To Know!

CHARLOTTE GIBBS

© **Copyright 2024 - All rights reserved.**

The content contained within this book may not be reproduced, duplicated, or transmitted without direct written permission from the author or the publisher.

Under no circumstances will any blame or legal responsibility be held against the publisher or author for any damages, reparation, or monetary loss due to the information contained within this book, either directly or indirectly.

Legal Notice:

This book is copyright-protected. It is only for personal use. You cannot amend, distribute, sell, use, quote, or paraphrase any part of the content within this book without the consent of the author or publisher.

Disclaimer Notice:

Please note the information contained within this document is for educational and entertain-ment purposes only. Every effort has been executed to present accurate, up-to-date, reliable, and complete information. No warranties of any kind are declared or implied. Readers ac-knowledge that the author is not engaged in rendering legal, financial, medical, or professional advice. The content within this book has been derived from various sources. Please consult a licensed professional before attempting any techniques outlined in this book.

By reading this document, the reader agrees that under no circumstances is the author respon-sible for any losses, direct or indirect, that are incurred as a result of the use of the information contained within this document, including, but not limited to, errors, omissions, or inaccuracies.

Table Of Contents

Introduction—Cluck Yeah for Chickens!..3

CHAPTER 1
Types and Breeds of Chickens 5
Laying Hens: Egg-cellent Layers! 6
Meat Chickens: The Feathered Racers! 7
Dual-Purpose Chickens: Double the Fun!.......................................7
Chicken Breeds: Feathers for Every Fan! 8

CHAPTER 2
Chicken Anatomy 11
Chicken Feathers: Feathers for Flight (Sort Of!) 12
Chicken Combs and Wattles: Those Funny Red Things 13
How Chickens Eat: Munching Machines..15
How Eggs Are Made: The Eggcellent Journey 15

CHAPTER 3
Chicken Housing..18
Chicken Coops: Finding the Perfect Place 19
Beyond the Coop: Building a Backyard Paradise.........................20
Keeping Your Chickens Thriving: Happy Hens, Healthy Hens! 21
Coop Comforts: Making Life Cluck-tacular! 23
Chicken Coop Safety Tips..23

CHAPTER 4
Chicken Diet and Nutrition 26
What Chickens Eat: A Menu Fit for a Feathered Friend 27
Feeding Time: A Chicken's Eating Schedule 29
H2O: The Essential Ingredient 29

CHAPTER 5
Chicken Behavior 32
The Flock: Living the Coop Life! 33
Communicating: The Cluck, Cluck, Chatterbox! 33
Foraging: The Great Grub Hunt! 34
Bathing: The Amazing Dust Bath! 35
Sleeping: Cozy Coop Critters 35

CHAPTER 6
Chicken Reproduction and Life Cycle 37
The Egg: How Chicks Get Started 39
From Egg to Chick: The Hatching Countdown! 40
Growing Up: From Chick to Chicken! 40
Motherly Love: The Power of a Broody Hen 41

CHAPTER 7
Common Chicken Health Concerns 43
Feeling Sick: Uh, Oh, My Chicken Isn't Feeling Well! 45
Staying Safe: Preventing Problems Before They Start 46
Going to the Vet: When to Call the Coop Doc 47

Conclusion 49

COLORING FUN: LET'S BRING CHICKENS TO LIFE! 52

Introduction—Cluck Yeah for Chickens!

Welcome to Chickens for Kids!

Have you ever heard a funny little "cluck" coming from your backyard? That might be a chicken saying hello! Chickens are feathered friends that people have been taking care of for a super long time, even longer than your grandparents' grandparents!

These clucking companions are pretty special. They give us yummy eggs for breakfast and tasty chicken for dinner. Plus, their fluffy feathers come in all sorts of amazing colors, from bright white to shiny black, and even speckled like chocolate chip cookies!

But wait, there's more! Chickens are full of surprises. They're curious and like to explore, they love to chat with each other in their own special language (we'll learn some of their words!), and they can even be quite social.

Ready to learn all about the secrets of these amazing birds? By the end of this book, you'll be a chicken whisperer, knowing all about how they look and act and why they're such important feathery friends!

CHAPTER 1
Types and Breeds of Chickens

All Shapes and Sizes: A Feathery Flock!

LAYING HENS: EGG-CELLENT LAYERS!

Did you know there are hundreds of different types of chickens? It's true! Just like people come in all shapes and sizes, so do chickens. But some chickens are superstars at a very special job: laying eggs! These champions are called laying hens, and they can lay one egg almost every day; that's like a magic trick they perform for us!

Meet the Rhode Island Red: Imagine a chicken with feathers as red as a fire truck! That's the Rhode Island Red, a popular laying hen known for her big, brown eggs that are perfect for breakfast scrambles.

Red and ready to rock—meet the Rhode Island rooster and hen!

The Leghorn's Pearly Whites: Look for a chicken with feathers as white as a pearl! That's a Leghorn, another superstar laying hen. Her eggs are usually white or lightly tinted and perfect for fluffy pancakes.

The Plymouth Rock Barricade: These chickens are named after a famous rock in the USA, but their feathers are anything but rock-like! Plymouth Rocks come in several colors, like barred black and white (imagine a zebra!), and are known for laying lots of medium-brown eggs.Meat Chickens: The Feathered Racers!

Not all chickens are built for laying eggs. Some are sleek and speedy, zipping around the coop like feathered race cars. These chickens are built for growing big and strong, and they're called meat chickens. They might not lay quite as many eggs as laying hens, but they sure do grow fast!

MEAT CHICKENS: THE FEATHERED RACERS!!

Not all chickens are built for laying eggs. Some are sleek and speedy, zipping around the coop like feathered race cars. These chickens are built for growing big and strong, and they're called meat chickens. They might not lay quite as many eggs as laying hens, but they sure do grow fast!

DUAL-PURPOSE CHICKENS: DOUBLE THE FUN!

Believe it or not, some chickens are like super chickens with two amazing talents! These are called dual-purpose chickens. They can be pretty good at both laying eggs and growing big! It's like having a superpower that lets you be good at drawing and singing at the same time! Some popular dual-purpose breeds include:

- **Wyandottes:** These friendly chickens come in many colors, with feathers that look like they've been neatly laced together. They're known for laying medium-brown eggs and having a calm personality.

- **New Hampshires:** These reddish-brown chickens are another great dual-purpose breed. They lay light brown eggs and are curious explorers, always pecking around to see what they can find.

CHICKEN BREEDS: FEATHERS FOR EVERY FAN!

We haven't even talked about the most eye-catching part of a chicken: its feathers! Chickens come in all sorts of amazing colors, from bright white to shiny black and even speckled like chocolate

Two Silky pals hanging out and fluffing around!

chip cookies! Some chickens even have feathers with cool patterns, like stripes or spots. Here are a couple of especially interesting breeds:

- **Silkies:** These fluffy chickens have feathers that feel more like fur than feathers, making them look like cuddly chicks all grown up! They come in many colors and are known for being very social butterflies.

- **Cochin:** Imagine a chicken with a feathery mane and beard, just like a tiny lion! That's the Cochin, a breed known for its incredibly fluffy feathers that come in white, black, and even buff (a light yellow color).So, next time you see a chicken, take a good look! You might be seeing a fluffy egg-laying machine, a speedy feathered friend, or maybe even a champion in both! Isn't the feathery world amazing?

Bonus Facts!

- Chickens are birds that have been domesticated for thousands of years!

- There are more chickens in the world than any other bird species.

- The scientific name for the chicken is Gallus gallus domesticus. How interesting!

- The longest recorded flight of a chicken lasted for 13 seconds.

- They are not the greatest at flying, but hey! They are fast! Chickens can run at speeds of up to 9 miles per hour.

CHAPTER 2
Chicken Anatomy

Cracking the Chicken Code: A Look Inside!

We've learned about all the different types of chickens, but what about the amazing parts that make them who they are? Buckle up because we're about to crack the chicken code and explore their fascinating anatomy!

CHICKEN FEATHERS: FEATHERS FOR FLIGHT (SORT OF!)

Chickens have some of the most stunning outfits in the animal kingdom! Their feathers come in all sorts of dazzling colors and patterns, from the classic white of a Leghorn to the jet black of a Black Australorp. Some breeds even have feathers with speckles like chocolate chip cookies, stripes like a racing car, or a poofy mane like a tiny lion (that's the Cochin breed!). But unlike their bird cousins who can soar through the sky, chickens are more grounded. Their feathers are lighter than you might think, almost like wearing a million tiny, fluffy threads. This lightness keeps them warm and comfy without being too heavy for them to flap their wings and take short bursts of flight, like hopping from the ground to a low fence post.

CHICKEN BEAKS: BUILT FOR BUSINESS

Next, let's talk about that beak! It might look funny, but a chicken's beak is a super tool. It's made of keratin, the same stuff that makes up our hair and nails. The top and bottom parts of the beak are hard and pointy, perfect for pecking at the ground for yummy seeds and insects. They can also use their beaks to tear up pieces of fruit and vegetables, break open nuts, and even groom their feathers. Imagine having a built-in shovel, fork, and comb all in one! The beak is also very sensitive, with lots of tiny nerves that help chickens feel what they're pecking at. This helps them find the tastiest morsels and avoid anything yucky.

CHICKEN COMBS AND WATTLES: THOSE FUNNY RED THINGS

Ever noticed those bright red things on a chicken's head? Those are called combs and wattles. They're kind of like a chicken's status symbol! Bigger combs and wattles usually mean it's a healthy adult chicken. These fleshy bits also help chickens stay cool by letting out extra heat. Imagine them as tiny radiators on a hot day! Combs and wattles are more prominent on roosters (the male chickens) than on hens (the female chickens). In fact, a rooster's comb can even change color depending on his mood! It might turn a brighter red when he's excited or feeling threatened by another rooster.

Shiny feathers and a fancy strut—this Wyandotte's got style!

HOW CHICKENS EAT: MUNCHING MACHINES

Chickens don't have teeth, so how do they eat? It's all thanks to their strong beaks and a special part of their tummy called a gizzard! First, they use their beaks to peck at food. They can be quite picky eaters, scratching at the ground to find just the right morsel. They might eat seeds, grains, insects, worms, and even small pebbles. Once they find something tasty, they swallow it whole. But the journey doesn't end there!

The food travels down a long tube called the esophagus, which is like a slippery slide for their food. Then, it reaches the gizzard, which is a muscular pouch full of tiny pebbles the chicken has swallowed. These pebbles act like little rocks in a washing machine, tumbling the food around and breaking it down into smaller pieces. Since chickens don't have teeth to chew their food, the gizzard does all the hard work! After the gizzard, the food moves on to the intestines, where all the nutrients are absorbed into the chicken's body. Finally, anything leftover gets... well, let's just say it exits the other end!

HOW EGGS ARE MADE: THE EGGCELLENT JOURNEY

One of the coolest things about chickens is that they lay eggs! But how does this amazing feat happen? It all starts inside a special place in the chicken called the ovary, where tiny yolks are formed. The yolk is like the golden center of a sunny-side-up egg, and it's full of nutrients for the developing chick. The yolk travels down a long tube called the oviduct, which is like a magical assembly line. As the yolk travels, the oviduct adds a layer of thick, clear liquid called albumen (that's the egg white!) and then a protective coating called the shell membrane. Finally, the calcium carbonate shell is formed, making the egg nice and strong. The whole process takes about 24-26 hours, and at the end, the egg pops out of the chicken, ready for us to enjoy in all sorts of delicious ways!

This is just a sneak peek into the amazing world of chicken anatomy. In the next chapter, we'll explore how these feathered friends communicate and even take a peek at their super cool coop life!

Bonus Facts!

- Chickens are believed to be descendants of the red junglefowl from Southeast Asia.

- Chickens can see in color and have excellent daytime vision!

- These feathery friends are known to show empathy toward other chickens and even recognize human faces!

- The term "pecking order" comes from chickens; it refers to the social hierarchy within a group.

- Chickens are related to dinosaurs, crazy, right? They share some genetic similarities with their ancient ancestors.

CHAPTER 3
Chicken Housing

Coop Crazy: Designing a Dream Home for Your Feathered Friends!

So, you've learned all about the fantastic world of chickens – their different types, how they're built, and their fascinating way of life. Now, you might be wondering: how can I bring these clucking companions into my own backyard? Well, the first step is creating a happy and healthy home for them, and that's where amazing chicken coops come in!

CHICKEN COOPS: FINDING THE PERFECT PLACE

Chicken coops come in all shapes and sizes, from simple wooden structures to elaborate chicken palaces (okay, maybe not palaces, but definitely very comfy coops!). The best coop for you will depend on how many chickens you plan to have and how much space you have in your backyard. No matter the size, though, there are a few key features every coop should have:

- A Safe Haven: The coop should be a fortress for your feathered friends. Build it with strong, predator-proof materials like wood covered in hardware cloth (a special wire mesh), and make sure it has a secure door that closes tight with a latch. Think of it as a castle where no fox or raccoon can get through!

- Room to Roost: Chickens like to perch up high, feel safe, and survey their domain. Include sturdy roosting bars inside the coop, spaced a few inches apart. Imagine them as feathery bunk beds where your chickens can cuddle up for the night, practicing their best chicken snores.

- The Nesting Nook: Hens need a quiet, cozy place to lay their eggs. Create nesting boxes along the walls of the coop, with soft bedding like straw or wood shavings. Think of them as private maternity suites for your egg-laying chickens! Make sure the nesting boxes are placed off the ground and have a single entrance hole to keep the eggs safe and dark.

BEYOND THE COOP: BUILDING A BACKYARD PARADISE

A coop is important, but chickens also love spending time outdoors. That's why many people build runs attached to their coops. A run is like a big, fenced-in playground where chickens can unleash their inner explorers. Use sturdy chicken wire to create a secure enclosure, giving them plenty of space to scratch, peck, dust bathe, and chase each other around. You can even add some fun features to their outdoor space, like:

- **Climbing structures:** Logs, branches, and small ladders give chickens places to perch and survey their territory, feeling like kings and queens of their own little coop kingdom.

- **Dust bathing areas:** Chickens love to take dust baths to keep clean and free of pests. Provide a shallow pit filled with dry dirt or sand for them to roll around in.

- **Fresh greens and herbs:** Planting a small herb garden or scattering some chopped vegetables in the run gives your chickens a chance to enjoy some tasty treats and peck at fresh greens.

KEEPING YOUR CHICKENS THRIVING: HAPPY HENS, HEALTHY HENS!

Now that your chickens have a fantastic coop and run, it's time to discuss care! Taking care of chickens is pretty simple, but it's important to do it right to keep them happy and healthy. Here are some clucking good tips:

- **Breakfast, Lunch, and Dinner:** Chickens need a balanced diet of food and water just like us! There are special chicken feed mixes available that have all the nutrients they need to stay strong, lay lots of eggs (if they're hens), and grow big and healthy (if they're roosters). Don't forget to keep a fresh water source available at all times in a container that won't tip over easily. You can even add some fun things to their feeder, like chopped vegetables or a handful of mealworms, for a tasty treat.

- **Cleanliness is Next to Chickenliness:** Just like you wouldn't want to live in a messy house, chickens don't like dirty coops. Clean out their coop regularly, removing droppings and old bedding. This will help keep them healthy and prevent bad smells. You can even train your chickens to use a designated "bathroom" area in the run by filling it with deep litter like wood shavings.

- **Keeping the Coop Doc Away:** A healthy coop is a happy coop! There are simple things you can do to keep your chickens healthy, like regularly checking for signs of illness (like lethargy or lack of appetite) and providing them with a dust bathing area to help get rid of mites and other pests. You can also talk to your local vet about any concerns you might have and get advice on keeping your feathered friends healthy and thriving.

By following these tips and creating a loving home, you can enjoy the company of your feathered friends for years to come.

COOP COMFORTS: MAKING LIFE CLUCK-TACULAR!

There are a few extra things you can add to your chicken coop to make it even more comfortable and enriching for your feathered friends. Here are some ideas:

- **Lighting:** Chickens are natural early risers, waking up with the sunrise. To help them adjust to shorter winter days, you can install a timer-controlled light in the coop. This will give them a little extra morning sunshine and keep them happy and productive.

- **Ventilation:** Fresh air is important for your chickens' health. Make sure your coop has good ventilation, with windows or vents that allow air to circulate freely. However, avoid creating drafts that could make your chickens cold.

- **Entertainment:** Chickens can get bored, just like any pet. Provide them with some fun things to keep them occupied, like hanging toys made from rope, brightly colored balls, or even a small mirror (chickens love looking at their reflections!). You can also scatter some straw or hay in the run for them to peck through and explore.

CHICKEN COOP SAFETY TIPS

Keeping your chickens safe is a top priority. Here are some additional safety tips to remember:

- **Location, Location, Location:** Place your coop in a well-drained area that gets some sunshine but also has shade during the hottest part of the day. Make sure it's not too close to your house to avoid unpleasant coop smells.

- **Predator Patrol:** Chickens are prey animals, so it's important to protect them from predators like foxes, raccoons, and hawks. Build a secure coop with a strong door and bury hardware cloth around the perimeter of the run to create a barrier underground that predators can't dig through.

- **Winter Wonderland:** Chickens can handle cold weather pretty well, but it's important to make sure their coop is well-insulated to keep them warm during the winter. You can use straw bales, blankets, or even deep litter bedding to help insulate the walls and floor. Provide a source of heat, like a heat lamp set on a thermostat, if you live in a very cold climate.

By following these tips, you can create a fantastic coop and run that will be the envy of all the chickens in the neighborhood! Your feathered friends will have a safe, comfortable, and enriching place to live, and you'll get to enjoy the companionship of these funny, curious, and egg-cellent creatures.

Bonus Facts

- Have you ever seen an egg with double yolks? It's relatively rare, but some chickens can lay these special eggs.

- In some cultures, chickens are symbols of good luck and fertility.

- Chickens can sleep with one eye open and the other one closed.

- There's a breed of chicken that has black feathers, black skin, and even black internal organs. It's called Ayam Cemani.

- Sadly, chickens have been used for cockfighting, a practice that is now illegal in many countries because it's cruel to the animals.

CHAPTER 4
Chicken Diet and Nutrition

Chow Time! A Feathered Feast for Your Flock

Chickens may not be picky eaters, but they sure do love a good meal! In this chapter, we'll crack open the secrets of chicken nutrition and explore what keeps these feathery friends happy and healthy.

WHAT CHICKENS EAT: A MENU FIT FOR A FEATHERED FRIEND

Chickens are omnivores, which means they enjoy a smorgasbord of both plants and animals. Their ideal diet is a balanced mix that provides all the nutrients they need to grow strong, lay eggs (if they're hens), and strut their stuff around the coop. Here's a closer look at the key ingredients in a chicken's clucking good menu:

- **Grains for Energy:** Grains like corn, wheat, and oats are the foundation of a chicken's diet. They provide a steady stream of energy to fuel their busy days of scratching, pecking, and exploring. Most chicken owners opt for commercially prepared chicken feed, a balanced blend of these grains and other important nutrients. These mixes come in different varieties depending on the age and needs of your chickens. For example, chicks have different dietary requirements than adult hens or roosters.

- **Veggie Power:** Chickens love the taste (and vitamins!) of fresh vegetables and fruits. Think of them as healthy snacks packed with essential nutrients. Tomatoes, chopped lettuce, carrots, and even berries are all welcome additions to their diet. But remember, chickens don't have teeth, so chop everything up into bite-sized pieces to avoid choking hazards. Start with small quantities at first to see what your chickens like to avoid any digestive upset.

- **Protein for Strength:** Just like us, chickens need protein to build strong muscles and healthy feathers. Protein helps chicks grow, and adult chickens maintain their bodies. While commercial feed provides some protein, you can also supplement their diet with sources like mealworms, crickets, or even a small amount of cooked, shredded chicken (of course!). These protein-rich treats are like power-ups for your feathered friends.

FEEDING TIME: A CHICKEN'S EATING SCHEDULE

Chickens are early birds in more ways than one! As the sun rises, they'll be eager for breakfast. This is typically the time for their biggest meal of the day, usually consisting of a generous helping of chicken feed. Throughout the day, they'll graze on leftover feed, peck at greens and insects they find in their run, and enjoy any treats you provide. Think of it as a constant snacking session fueled by curiosity and a love for tasty morsels. As evening approaches and the sun starts to set, they'll have a final dinner of chicken feed to keep them full through the night.

H_2O: THE ESSENTIAL INGREDIENT

Just like for us humans, water is essential for a chicken's health. They need clean, fresh water to stay hydrated, regulate their body temperature, and keep their digestive system working properly. Dehydration can lead to a variety of health problems in chickens, so it's crucial to make sure they always have access to a clean water source.

Here are some tips for keeping your chickens hydrated:

- **Choose the Right Waterer:** There are different types of chicken waterers available, from simple gravity-fed dispensers to automatic watering systems. Choose one that's the right size for your flock and won't tip over easily.

- **Location, Location, Location:** Place the waterer in a shaded area of the coop or run to keep the water cool and fresh. Avoid placing it near feeders where it could get contaminated with food scraps.

- **Fresh and Clean:** Clean the waterer regularly to remove any algae or debris that could build up. This will help keep the water fresh and appealing to your chickens.

- **Winter Considerations:** If you live in a cold climate, you might need to take extra steps to ensure your chickens have access to unfrozen water during the winter months. There are heated waterers available, or you can simply swap out the water more frequently to prevent freezing.

The right food and water are the cornerstones of good chicken health. By providing your chickens with a balanced diet and fresh water, you're helping them stay strong, healthy, and ready to lay lots of eggs (if they're hens) or crow proudly (if they're roosters). In the next chapter, we'll take a heartwarming journey into the world of baby chicks, exploring how these adorable balls of fluff hatch and grow into the amazing chickens we know and love!

Bonus Facts

- Chickens has been kept as pets for years, they are great companions, and they help get rid of insects in the garden!

- The Brahma chicken is one of the largest breeds; the hens can weigh up to 12 pounds.

- Chickens can be trained! You can teach them to respond to their names and even perform simple tricks.

- The term "chicken" is sometimes used to describe someone who is afraid or timid.

- Some famous cartoon chickens are Foghorn Leghorn from Looney Tunes and Chicken Little from Disney.

CHAPTER 5
Chicken Behavior

Clucking Secrets: Decoding Chicken Talk!

Chickens might not speak our language, but they sure have a lot to say! In this chapter, we'll crack the code on chicken behavior and discover how these feathered friends communicate and live together.

THE FLOCK: LIVING THE COOP LIFE!

Chickens are social butterflies. They love hanging out with other chickens in a group called a flock. Imagine a big family of feathered friends, all clucking and pecking around together. There's a pecking order in the flock, which is like a set of rules about who's boss. The chicken at the top of the pecking order (usually the biggest, strongest hen) gets to eat first, take the best dust bathing spots, and has bragging rights in the coop. But don't worry, there's usually not too much fighting. Chickens use a special kind of body language to communicate who's in charge, like puffing out their feathers or raising their combs.

COMMUNICATING: THE CLUCK, CLUCK, CHATTERBOX!

Chickens might not have words like us, but they have a whole vocabulary of clucks, cackles, and peeps to chat with each other. A loud cluck might mean "Danger!" while a soft purr could mean "I found a yummy worm!" Roosters are especially chatty. Their loud crowing is like a wake-up call for the whole coop, letting everyone know the sun is up.

Colorful rooster with a clucking cheer—he's got the best wake-up song!

FORAGING: THE GREAT GRUB HUNT!

Chickens love to spend their days foraging for food. They're like feathered detectives, scratching at the ground with their strong legs and beaks to uncover hidden treasures – juicy worms, wiggling grubs, and tasty seeds. They also love pecking at plants and even the occasional lizard or small insect. It's like a giant game of hide-and-seek for yummy snacks!

BATHING: THE AMAZING DUST BATH!

Chickens might not have bathtubs, but they have a special way to keep clean – the dust bath! They find a patch of dry dirt and then wiggle and roll around in it, fluffing up their feathers and sending dust flying. This dust bath helps get rid of mites and other tiny pests that might be bugging them (literally!). It's like a spa day for chickens, leaving them feeling squeaky clean and ready to face the day.

SLEEPING: COZY COOP CRITTERS

At the end of a long day of chatting, eating, and dust bathing, chickens need their beauty sleep. They roost together at night, usually perching on high places like branches or bars in their coop. This helps them feel safe from predators and keeps them warm through the night. Some chickens even snuggle together for extra warmth, like a feathery cuddle puddle!

By understanding chicken behavior, we can learn to appreciate these amazing birds even more. In the next chapter, we'll explore the fascinating world of baby chicks and discover how these little balls of fluff grow into the clucking chickens we know and love!

Bonus Facts

- The phrase "Don't count your chickens before they hatch" means that you shouldn't assume something will happen until it actually does.

- Chickens love their home! They are able to find their way back to their coop from long distances.

- Chicken breeding is very common, especially for meat production (broilers) and egg production (layers.)

- Roosters perform a "courtship dance" called tidbitting. This is meant to attract hens and impress them!

- You can use the phrase "running around like a headless chicken" to refer to someone who is very disorganized!

CHAPTER 6
Chicken Reproduction and Life Cycle

The Miracle of Life: Hatching a Feathery Family!

Chickens are amazing creatures, and one of the coolest things about them is how they reproduce. In this chapter, we'll crack the code on chicken reproduction and explore the fascinating journey from egg to adult chicken!

THE EGG: HOW CHICKS GET STARTED

For a chick to hatch, it all starts with a very special egg. But how does this amazing feat happen? The story begins inside a female chicken, called a hen, in a place called the ovary. Here, tiny yolks, which are like the golden centers of fried eggs, are formed. The yolk is full of nutrients that will nourish the developing chick.

Inside the hen, this tiny yolk begins its journey. It travels down a long tube called the oviduct. Think of this oviduct as a busy factory. As the yolk travels, the oviduct gets to work! First, it adds a thick, clear liquid called albumen, which becomes the egg white. Next, it coats the yolk and albumen in a thin, protective layer called the shell membrane. Finally, the oviduct creates a hard outer shell of calcium carbonate to keep everything safe and secure. This amazing process takes about 24-26 hours, and at the end, a complete egg emerges from the hen, ready for the next stage of its adventure – hatching a chick!

But how does a yolk turn into a chick? That's where the rooster comes in! If a rooster mates with a hen, the egg yolk can become fertilized. This means that a special cell from the rooster joins with the yolk, starting the process of chick development. If the egg is not fertilized, it will still be a perfect egg for us to eat, but it won't develop into a chick.

FROM EGG TO CHICK: THE HATCHING COUNTDOWN!

If the egg is fertilized, something amazing starts to happen inside. The fertilized yolk starts to divide and grow, forming an embryo – that's the tiny chick in its early stages. Over the next 21 days, the embryo grows bigger and stronger, developing all the parts it needs to become a chick, like tiny wings, legs, and a beak. The chick also uses the yolk sac for food as it grows.

As hatching day approaches, the chick starts to peck at the inside of the egg with its little beak. This pecking helps create a crack in the shell. Finally, with a burst of effort, the chick pushes its way out of the egg and into the world! This process is called hatching.

GROWING UP: FROM CHICK TO CHICKEN!

Baby chickens, called chicks (no surprise there!), are adorable balls of fluff. They are wet from hatching and need some time to dry off before they can walk around. But they don't need to find food right away! Nature has given them a special leftover from the egg called the yolk sac, which provides them with nutrients for the first day or two of their lives.

Once they're dry and fluffy, chicks are ready to explore the world! They follow their mother hen around, learning how to find food, preen their feathers, and take dust baths. The mother hen keeps them warm and safe under her wings and even teaches them how to communicate using special chick chirps!

Over the next few weeks, chicks grow quickly. Their feathers start to come in, and they learn to become more independent. By about six months old, they are considered adults and are ready to start laying eggs (if they are hens) or crowing (if they are roosters).

MOTHERLY LOVE: THE POWER OF A BROODY HEN

Some hens have a special instinct to become mothers, and they're called broody hens. A broody hen will sit on a nest of eggs (fertilized or not) for long periods of time, keeping them warm with her body heat. This helps the chicks develop inside the eggs. Broody hens are also very protective of their chicks once they hatch. They'll cluck softly to them, keep them warm under their wings, and fiercely defend them from any danger.

Chicken reproduction is a fascinating process, and it's a reminder of the amazing miracle of life. From a tiny egg to a fluffy chick and then to a full-grown chicken, the journey is incredible. In the next chapter, we'll explore the amazing world of different chicken breeds, from the fluffy giants to the sleek and speedy birds. Get ready to meet a whole flock of feathered friends!

Bonus Facts

- Chickens have been used in therapy programs for their calming effect on humans.

- "Cock-a-doodle-doo" is the term used for the sound that a rooster makes to announce the dawn. Have you ever heard it?

- A rooster is also called a cockerel.

- The color of a chicken's eggshell depends on its breed. This is why we see white eggs, brown eggs, some blue, or even greenish!

- Chickens have a great sense of time, and they are able to predict when it's time to roost (go to sleep) based on the position of the sun!

CHAPTER 7
Common Chicken Health Concerns

Keeping Your Feathered Friends Fit

Red and ready to rock—meet the Rhode Island rooster and hen!

Just like us, chickens can sometimes get sick or injured. The good news is that by following good coop hygiene, providing a healthy diet, and keeping an eye on your flock, you can help prevent many common chicken health problems. In this chapter, we'll learn about some of the most common issues chickens face and how to keep your feathered friends happy and healthy.

FEELING SICK: UH, OH, MY CHICKEN ISN'T FEELING WELL!

How can you tell if your chicken is under the weather? Here are some signs to watch out for:

- **Loss of appetite:** If your chicken isn't interested in their food, it could be a sign of illness.

- **Lethargy:** A healthy chicken is an active chicken. If your chicken is listless and doesn't seem interested in exploring or scratching, it could be a sign of something wrong.

- **Unusual droppings:** Healthy chicken droppings are usually brown with a white urate sac. Diarrhea, bloody droppings, or discolored droppings can all be signs of illness.

- **Respiratory problems:** If your chicken is wheezing, coughing, or has a runny nose, it could be a sign of a cold or respiratory infection.

STAYING SAFE: PREVENTING PROBLEMS BEFORE THEY START

The best way to keep your chickens healthy is to prevent them from getting sick in the first place. Here are some tips:

- **Cleanliness is Next to Chickenliness:** A clean coop is a healthy coop! Regularly remove droppings, old bedding, and any uneaten food to prevent the buildup of bacteria and parasites.

- **A Balanced Diet:** Ensure your chickens get the nutrients they need by providing them with high-quality chicken feed and fresh vegetables and fruits.

- **Fresh Water is Essential:** Always keep clean, fresh water available for your chickens.

- **Pest Patrol:** Parasites like mites and worms can make chickens sick. Use preventative measures like dust baths and diatomaceous earth to control pests in the coop and run.

- **Stress Less, Cluck More:** Stress can weaken a chicken's immune system and make them more susceptible to illness. Provide your chickens with a safe and comfortable environment with plenty of space to roam and hiding spots to feel secure.

GOING TO THE VET: WHEN TO CALL THE COOP DOC

If you notice any signs of illness in your chickens, it's important to take action. Here's when to call a veterinarian who specializes in poultry:

- **Severe symptoms:** If your chicken is experiencing severe symptoms like difficulty breathing, bleeding, or seizures, seek veterinary help immediately.

- **No improvement:** If your chicken has been sick for a few days and isn't getting better with home care, it's time to call the vet.

- **Mysterious illness:** If you're unsure what's wrong with your chicken, a vet can help diagnose the problem and recommend treatment.

Taking your chicken to the vet might seem daunting, but most vets are happy to help feathered patients. Here's what to expect:

- **The Exam:** The vet will ask you about your chicken's symptoms and history. They will then perform a physical exam to check your chicken's overall health.

- **Diagnosis and Treatment:** Based on the exam and any tests that might be needed, the vet will diagnose the problem and recommend treatment. This might include medication, dietary changes, or wound care.

- **Home Recovery:** The vet will give you instructions on how to care for your chicken at home while they recover.

By being observant and taking preventative measures, you can help keep your chickens healthy and happy. But if your feathered friend does get sick, don't hesitate to seek professional help from a veterinarian. In the next chapter, we'll meet the fascinating world of different chicken breeds, from the gentle giants to the sassy chanteuses of the coop!

Bonus Facts!

- Roosters have colorful feathers and often larger combs and wattles compared to hens.

- Chickens have personalities; some are bold and curious, others are more shy and cautious.

- A famous comical rooster character is Hei Hei, from Moana. He's very amusing and clueless!

- The Silkie chicken is a beautiful breed known for its fur-like feathers and its black skin and bones.

- In many places around the world, chickens are thought to bring good luck and happiness to families who raise them.

CONCLUSION

Chickens are more than just egg-laying machines (although fresh eggs are a pretty awesome perk!). They are intelligent, social creatures with unique personalities. They can be curious and playful, sometimes even a little mischievous! Raising chickens can be a rewarding experience, and it allows you to connect with nature and learn about these amazing birds. Chickens play an important role in our world. They provide us with delicious eggs, a source of protein that can be enjoyed in countless ways. They also help control insect populations by scratching and pecking in the soil. And let's not forget the joy they bring! Chickens can be fun companions, and their antics can provide endless entertainment. This is why it is very important to take good care of them. The next time you see a chicken, take a moment to appreciate these remarkable creatures. From their fluffy feathers to their egg-laying abilities, chickens are truly clucking awesome! We think you're pretty amazing, too, for getting to the end of this book and becoming an expert on all things chickens!

COLORING FUN: LET'S BRING CHICKENS TO LIFE!

SPECIAL BONUS!

Want These 2 Books For FREE?

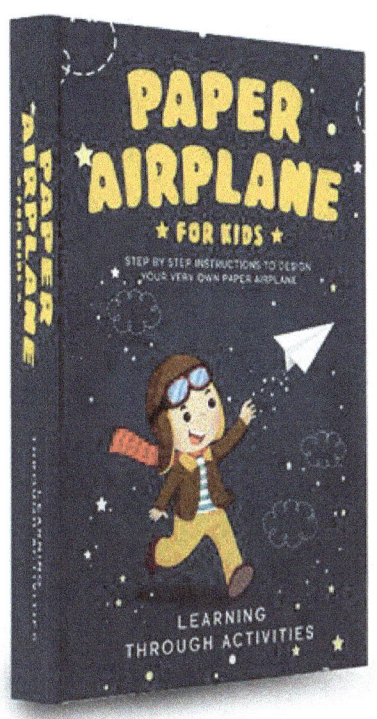 

Get **FREE**, unlimited access to these and all of our new kids books by joining our community!

Scan W/ Your Camera To Join!

www.ingramcontent.com/pod-product-compliance
Lightning Source LLC
Chambersburg PA
CBHW081627100526
44590CB00021B/3630